Exploring fifteen years of teaching, decades of religious questions and a lifetime of longing, Czaia both compresses time and elongates it for our benefit. His work is refreshingly honest, embodied, raw, vulnerable and ultimately hopeful, challenging us to claim our precious lives and show up for our communities.

– Ellie Roscher, author of *12 Tiny Things, Play Like a Girl* and
How Coffee Saved My Life

Zach Czaia is the most miraculous kind of artist: the teacher/ poet. How reassuring it is to know that the literary education of young people is in the hands of such a gifted wordsmith and such a tender-hearted teacher.

– Deborah Appleman, Professor of Educational Studies, Carleton College, and author of *Words No Bars Can Hold: Literacy Learning in Prison*

Welcome to knucklehead poetry: in a beautiful line, a propulsive stanza, and an apparently artless form, each poem thrills with the voice of a man trying to be a human being, a knucklehead his God is trying to aggravate into divine awareness, failures redeemed in memory—if not by time, then perhaps by the art of poetry itself.

– Scott Crider, Professor of English, The University of Dallas, and author of *The Office of Assertion: An Art of Rhetoric For the Academic Essay*

"Open your mouth," begins *Knucklehead*. Our scrappy speaker, at times named Knucklehead, teaches English literature to high school students, prays in a Catholic church, is a husband, was a missionary in Belize. Knucklehead makes meaning of his life and his choices through the lens of another knucklehead named Paul, the most human, controversial tentmaker in the Bible. Our poet's poems challenge author and reader to remain open as Jesus did. Here is a poet. Here is a citizen. Here is a knucklehead. Here is a prophet.

– Spencer Reece, author of *The Clerk's Tale* and
The Road to Emmaus

In *Knucklehead*, Czaia prompts us to seek unpolished diamonds in the dirt of our life, in the midst of a world that appears to have lost its centre. Whilst engaging us in life's struggles and failures, Czaia invites us to live out that existential tension of being there, but not quite, of hidden yet visible grace, of being home yet exiled, for the sake of valuing the gift of thisness in everyone and in everything, lest we remain confined to a reality punctuated by Czaia's words in the cry of Twain out of purgatory "We wish we had time [...] We have the wait for but we do not have time." *Knucklehead* mirrors our own vicissitudes, whether in a quaint town in Central America or in bustling municipalities like the Twin Cities, reminding us that we are all *cabeza dura* or knuckleheads, and that in our blindness, "if we would [only] understand what happened on the road to Damascus," we would come to the realization that the old is gone, and the new has come (cf. 2 Cor. 5:17), and that there is power and grace even in the stones that make us stumble.

– David Nicolas Ruiz,
Belizean educator and story teller

The poems in Zach Czaia's Knucklehead address the struggle of becoming wise. They are open-hearted and lucid, tender and wry. "I want to return to the moment of my belief / though the moment of my disillusionment is good too," the poet writes about his brother tricking him into eating leaves when they were children. Wisdom proverbially knocks Czaia to the ground as Saul was on the road to Damascus, and comes through the struggles, delights, and occasional grief of teaching high school and entering into marriage. Czaia ends his book still a knucklehead — aren't we all? — but he exits more sure of love, grace, and a God who "lives like birds or trees, / lives like branches growing, / is shade, is cool — is free."

– Katrina Vandenberg, author of *The Alphabet Not Unlike the World* and *Atlas: Poems*

KNUCKLEHEAD

poems

Zach Czaia

NODIN PRESS

The following poems have been published or accepted for publication prior to this book's release:
"If You Would Understand What Happened On the Road To Damascus" with *Presence*
"Two Letters From Luke" with *Bearings Online Journal*
"Dante! Dante!" with *Dappled Things*
"I Don't Want To Write A Poem For My Dead Students" with *NCTE Journal*
"An Aesthetic" with *Tinderbox Poetry Journal*
"Public Works" with *Thimble Literary Magazine*
"Mark Twain, From Purgatory" with *Talking Stick*
"Saint Paul Talks Strategy" with *Ekstasis Magazine*
"The First Snowfall in Minneapolis" with *EcoTheo Review*

Cover art by Maceo Montoya: "She Said She Would Call the Wind"

ISBN: 978-1-947237-39-1

9 8 7 6 5 4 3 2 1

Library of Congress Control Number: 2021948057

Published by

Nodin Press
5114 Cedar Lake Road
Minneapolis, MN   55416

Printed in U.S.A.

To my students

CONTENTS

I

II

I

...*And when we were all fallen to the earth, I heard a voice speaking unto me, and saying in the Hebrew tongue, Saul, Saul, why persecutest thou me? It is hard for thee to kick against the pricks...*

— *Acts 26:14*

IF YOU WOULD UNDERSTAND WHAT HAPPENED ON THE ROAD TO DAMASCUS

Open your mouth. Your tongue,
put it out. Let it wait.
Let it wait till it is
dry and cool. Let it wait

past the point, long past it,
when you think, *here I am,*
a grown man standing here
like a child. Then, your hands,

hold them out, too. Open
them, and let them wait, too.
If you would understand,
want to know what I knew,

you would wait, hold yourself
for as long as you can
in this way, till the voice
speaks. And you know the man,

though you cannot yet place
from where. You know that voice.
And only now open
your eyes. And now the choice

is made, though now you see him,
now you are on the ground...
Why? Why? He asks *Why?* All
why, it is the only sound

you can hear. Take it in.
You know you must answer
but you don't know how to.
Your mouth is a dancer

without music, without
rhythm, without a clue
of how to move. You try—
the words die within you.

He is no guide. He's gone
and you are left with *why?*
It echoes in the dark.
It settles down to die,

It penetrates your bones—
you feel it in the thud—
why beat *why* beat *why* beat *why* beat
in the heart, in the blood.

He lives and you know it,
lives like birds or trees,
lives like branches growing,
is shade, is cool—is free.

THE POET CONSIDERS HIS MARRIAGE

Marriage has made him want to finish
more of his sentences. Has made him
want to start more, too,
find out how they end.

The Poet thinks, *maybe this one job,*
I can do this one well.

He plans for her surprise birthday party.
He calls some of her friends, texts others.
Emails some. Talks to her parents,
thinks about a place she might like to eat.

The Poet was not born into a world of pain.
He is almost 35 years old,
has never been to war,
still has both of his parents.

So why does he write this poem?
He looks at others who need to write
and thinks, *yes, but why me?*
Why do I need
the next line?

Marriage has taught him to wait:
for storms in good weather
and good weather in storms,
salt and sugar,
the old clichés.

He's planning her surprise party!
And he shouldn't be surprised
that sometimes this makes him feel
like he deserves a pat on the back.

Marriage has taught the Poet he's not nearly as good
as he thought he was. For example,
he ate the last bit of left-over pasta
last night, and there was nothing left for her,
and do you know what he thought? He thought,
yes, but I am planning this surprise birthday party.

He has to have a beer at the end of the day.
He has to have coffee at the start.
He tells himself if he doesn't ignore the small simple facts
perhaps then he will discover something profound.
How is that working out for him, you ask?

Sometimes he's scared of powerful women.
Like his wife. When she yells at him, he is afraid,
tries to crawl in to a hole in himself,
a place in his history, way back,
like when he was a little child
trying to escape the wrath of his mother.
He knows this is not very mature.

He is planning this surprise party
because she once told him she wanted one.
She said, "Wouldn't it be great if I could have
a surprise birthday party? With all the friends
from my life?" She said it twice.
The Poet said, "Duly noted," and he did note it.

During their last fight, when she said
You never think of me, and he said that's not true,
and she demanded evidence,
he said he couldn't, he said, "It's not something I can talk
    about."
He was very proud of himself then.
You know what he was thinking about?
This surprise birthday party
he's planning for her. You see,
he's not such a bad guy after all.
He can keep a secret.

TWO LETTERS FROM LUKE

i.
You ask me why? Why smooth out his rough spots?
Why not show the flaws of the man entire?
I gave Paul another Gospel? I thought
the message mattered more. I think Empire
taken over from the inside—new King.
I think bold doesn't have to be stupid,
think we've got a bell we're going to ring
in different ways in different places. Cupid
knows: you pick a certain kind of arrow
for a certain kind of person. Same here.
God knows the way to the heart of a Pharaoh:
plagues for him, a breath for us—it came here
like the strike of a snake, wings of a dove
spread wide. All nothing…if we have not love.

ii.
And it's all nothing if we have not love.
And these little pods of people gathered,
and this tentative peace we're talking of,
and the way we say as if it mattered—
God became man…
                Yes, we have made mistakes
and you deserve to be the first to know
that nothing's happening here, no big break.
He is stuck in a little room in Rome
and the Emperor isn't listening,
and the leaders of the synagogue came,
heard his piece, and they aren't listening,
and we sit, pray and listen to the rain.
Maybe God's playing us a little song?
Drip. Love. Drop. Love. Drip…or maybe we're wrong.

DANTE! DANTE!

They used to call out
when they saw me on the streets
of their village.
I was 23 years old,
they were 17.

Dante! Dante!
they called
because that was the book
I made them read,
all 33 *pinche* cantos
of the inferno.

I can see them still,
all 33 boys
from my third form class
in Benque, Belize.
Heads bent low
over the packets of poetry.
From seat to seat
I moved in the silence,
looking over their shoulders
as they read
or pretended to.

Dante! Dante!
they called.
Maybe they hated him
but I want to think I was okay.
Okay, this gringo doing his year
of service. Okay

in a limited sort of way.
Okay, in the I came, I saw
I had my world
kicked open kind of way. Okay,
in the I could pack my bags
and go home kind of way,
which after a year
I did.

Dante, Dante!
they called to me
while they ran past
hopping over rocks
on the banks of the Mopan River.
I swam too
but not as fast.
I swam alone
not like them,
in schools, those seventeen-year-old boys
from my class now the same age
as my wife. That's the funny way
of time.

The funny way of poetry
makes memory unlimited.
In those days
I didn't know to hunger
for my wife
because I hadn't met her.
I didn't know to hunger
for justice
because I hadn't tasted it.
I was thin
as November ice. I knew nothing

and was a teacher.
I was a teacher and I knew nothing
for myself
so I taught you,
Dante.

Dante,
exile makes you sound too fancy.
But you were kicked out of your home.
You couldn't go back.
You were a refugee.
You know
better than anyone
just because everyone
knows everyone
doesn't make anyone
safe.

The dogs of Benque
were ragged things. At night
walking home from the school
I didn't know who to be more afraid of,
their flashing teeth and hoarse barking
or the men by their sides,
in the shadows, cradling their beer,
a glaze over their eyes
that sometimes sparked
if I looked at them
and I'd pick up my pace,
and my heart would thump
a new quick beat
in the dark.

Dante, Dante—
Flash forward 10 years
from Benque,
from my 3rd formers, the Mopan River.
See me writing my own poem now.
It is as judgy as myself,
as full of me.
I see my archbishop's deputy
chewing on his master's brain
as your Ugolino
chewed Ruggieri.
I thought I was very clever
to use your words
to paint my church.
I liked throwing the judgement stone.
My picture was important work
I told myself
though a day of listening
to the kids I teach
was better for my soul
than a thousand poems like that one.

Dante, Dante—
All my life
judgement has been more real to me
than jesus.
Even though I know
his blood drops down
even in to hell,
even though
when he was crucified
the very rocks,
cracked in two

and three
and four.

Dante, Dante—
On one of the last days of class
we read your 33rd canto,
my 3rd formers and me—
Ugolino confessing his sin to you,
painting the scene.
How he was trapped in the tower
with his little boys,
how he watched them starve
one by one,
how he ate them up with his own
mouth and teeth
before he died.
I read it aloud
because that was the way
they understood the words best.
I read it aloud
and cried
fat, wet tears
imagining that father,
and the hole
in his heart,
the coldness of the ice,
the love
that wasn't there

I DON'T WANT TO WRITE A POEM FOR MY DEAD STUDENTS

— for Diana & Chris

Just last June
I watched them both walk across the stage,
my dead students.
And once,
I taught them 9th grade English
while they were still alive,
breathing, walking, talking.

Someone drove a car
the wrong way down I-94
and killed them.
That's what happened.
My students killed.
My students? No—

When I remember Diana
memorizing
I Have a Dream
by Martin Luther King, Jr.,
when I see her standing in front
of her classmates, saying those words,
and her classmates hearing them—
that is not mine.
It is not mine
when she said *she*
wanted to work for that kind of justice TODAY.
It is not mine when Chris
was cutting up in class,
making his stupid jokes,
asking what it would take,

you know,
for me to 'forget'
that he hadn't done his homework today?

And I don't want to understand
the cosmic calculus of this.
And I don't want to think of forgiveness.
I just want to cry
big salty tears.
I want long sucking sobs.
I want this day to last a long, long time,
the first day Diana and Chris
weren't walking and talking
in the world,
but I was,
writing this poem.

– *September 27, 2017*

AN AESTHETIC

My brother once told me if I ate the leaves on the ground
they would turn to ice cream in my mouth.
I want to return to the moment of my belief
though the moment of my disillusionment is good, too,
the dirt and paper crunch of the maple leaves on my teeth and
tongue.

MARK TWAIN, FROM PURGATORY

To hell with T.S. Eliot and his love of Huck.
Toni Morrison is right about my book.
They should have kept going down the river.
I regret the way it ended.

In Purgatory do you think all of us dead white writers
are smoking and drinking ourselves into a sweet nostalgia?
We are not.

There is nothing for us but the patience of a new day,
the stroke of it off God's palette.

One day our eyes will open and we will be younger,
in the dawn again, having forgot what made us
avoid the gaze of the one looking at us—
my Jim! my God, what made me flee...

We wish we had time, which you have.
We have the wait for
but we do not have time.

BEATRICE SPEAKS HER TRUTH

He never mentions seeing *me* in Hell.
The teachers or friends whose stories he tells,
the bishops or statesmen who bend his ear—
they strut on the page; they flaunt and they sneer;
their songs shine down through the years like water:
the saved get God; damned, remembered better.
And I went to Hell for him, for his soul.
I was on the riverbank, watching Charon pole
the poets through the mud. I went to Hell.
When the gusts of lusts tossed and gonged him like a bell,
I was there. And *I* caught him when he swooned.
When his rivals turned the knife in his wound—
'You'll always be exile, now,"—I was there.
My hand made the pain something he could bear.

I walked in the footsteps that Virgil left,
watched them sleep, my watching they never guessed.
When they woke, I followed—they never knew,
to the ice, to the place where pain's always new.
Heard traitors tell tales, and saw Dante's tears
wash his face clean until his skin shone clear.
After Brutus, after Judas, ready,
he was ready; down the devil's legs, said he
found a passage through and up and out
of Hell. It's true they came to me, no doubt
thinking I was waiting. But I do not wait.
I live. I listen. And it's never too late
to revise the story of his life, and yours—
the mountain awaits us. Also, the stars.

KNUCKLEHEAD

I can still see the sneer on your freshman face,
hear the Spanish you spoke with brutal grace:

Chingate, pendejo, rolling off your tongue,
still see the stare I used to no effect—I was so young.

From other teachers I heard the same:
you liked to see us boil over. It was a game.

Go ahead, say, "I got to you!" Say, "Admit it,
Another month of me, you might have quit."

Maybe. But this isn't about settling scores.
This is me turning on lights, opening doors.

"I survived you," is ugly, but so is forgive,
so is, "I've learned so much." What is this,

then, this thing in my lap on the train?
Is this a poem? I get on. I'll get off again.

Western. Montrose. The stops pass me by.
Meanwhile I keep trying to pin it down. I

keep telling myself, *today will be
the day it clicks. You'll see.*

I could say, Knucklehead, that you're a leaf,
could say, we teachers, conductors, we're the trees.

I could say we watch you fall.
But none of that's it, not at all.

What you are now I'll never see,
and the thoughts, the words you kept from me

remain your own. My truth? I'm still reaching
for something lost when I left teaching.

If you find it, Knucklehead, finish my poem.
And tell me how *your* life has come home,

and what you grieve and do not grieve,
and all you love and do not leave.

II

By the grace of God I am what I am, and his grace to me was not without effect.

–1 Corinthians 15:10

THE KNUCKLEHEAD THROUGH THE AGES

In the beginning was the Word
which was God, and Light, etc.
but the Knucklehead didn't listen
and preferred the Darkness, all things
being equal, for it was quieter,
God didn't bother him there,
and he could drink his strong drink
in peace.

When the Prophets came with their fire
from God, the Knucklehead went
and started his own. It was not a fire
of Purity and Truth but an actual bonfire,
a place to rest and roast his chicken
and when the time came
to feast.

Moving forward several millennia…
(the Knucklehead impervious even
to the passage of time) we find him essentially
the same. The loves of his life
disclose their hearts
but the Knucklehead
does not know what to do.
When a thing does not fit
the world as the Knucklehead sees it,
the thing is thrown out and his world remains
unchanged.

So it was in the beginning,
is now
and ever shall be,
Knucklehead without end,
Amen.

STEPHEN & SAUL

While they were stoning Stephen, he prayed, "Lord Jesus, receive my spirit." Then he knelt down and cried out in a loud voice, "Lord, do not hold this sin against them." When he had said this, he died.

And Saul approved of their killing him.

—*Acts 7: 59 – 8:1*

I did.
I looked them in the eyes,
each man who threw a stone.
I congratulated them,
not with words but a
nod of the head, which let them know
I, too saw through this act,
I, too heard the recitation of history
as blasphemy—
Who was he
to step in to the tradition?
Who was he
to tell us
who we were?

I can still see
those rocks raining down,
and after, when his body
lay there,
broken, bleeding in the field,
I could not look
away from it.
Moments before
his face was shining,
his voice speaking.
Then we said,

'the end' to his story
and it was.

And it was.
We held with our hands
his life, those stones
we threw
thudded
face
back
kidney
chest.
They were power.
We took his life.

He said a thing
that disrupted our lives.
We took his.

He said,
One day Moses
woke up,
realized what *slave* meant,
realized *power*
and took the life
of an Egyptian.

One of the last things
he said.
And Moses fled.
And spent 40 years away
before he woke up again:

One day a burning bush.

One day I woke up too.
Realized.
Saw those stones
thudding again.
Saw the nods of the men
again
and the body of Stephen
in the field.

And fled, too
though I could not run
far enough.
The stones followed.
His voice followed.
In the wilderness
I lay down to sleep
with my murders.

I wrote my first epistle then.
I asked, why I alive
and he dead?
It's a question
He
never answered.

SAINT PAUL TALKS STRATEGY

So I went down to a potter's house, and there he was working at his wheel. Whenever the vessel he was making went wrong, as clay is apt to do in a potter's hand, he would remake it in a different shape, such as he thought suitable.

--Jeremiah 18:34

It's a go-to, I'll admit it,
the potter at his wheel. I say,
"I'm the stuff in his hands, the clay—
a pot gone wrong, he remade it,
remade me, my life." The prophet
knows more than I do. Hearts don't change
that much from age to age, the range
of feelings the same now as then.
We're all still waiting for the moment when
these hearts we carry don't feel so strange.

KNUCKLEHEAD'S REGRETS

Yes, they are
many.
No, I
can't count.

Mosquito bites
itch worse when
you scratch
them. Yes,

I have scratched them.

> — *After Amiri Baraka*

KNUCKLEHEAD'S FIRST FIGHT AS A TEACHER

Belizean Independence Day, 2005

Maybe I'd have been prepared if I ever had my own,
but I was quiet, never liked a mess.
When bullies took, I gave. They left me alone

with my shame. When *my* teachers noticed,
I denied it. It never got so bad
I needed to fight back. So my fists

I never used to punch when I got mad,
my knuckles and heart never tied up that way.
I never knew I'd miss what I never had.

I thought it would be a break that day:
we would walk the streets, we would wave and sing,
me and my class of boys on this holiday.

But after, in homeroom, waiting to be dismissed,
one of my Spanish-speaking kids flicked his yo-yo
into the leg of a Creole kid he dissed

and *that* kid flipped his desk over and now
they were bumping chests and I was between,
and they stared and I stared and wondered how

to make this go away. To make this scene
something better. "Watch the class," I said
to one I trusted. I got the Creole kid off scene.

"You can't do that," I told him then, didn't let
the kid explain. "Maestro, he was talking—"
"I don't care. Here, we don't fight. You got that?"

No nod. No nothing. And the kid was walking
away before I finished, so I called
the principal and went back to teaching

if you could call it that. And the kids all
could see I'd lost control of the room,
that I'd missed the words that passed while we'd walked.

I didn't know Spanish or Kriol. And soon
enough they'd try to settle more in class:
One day the Creole kid would lay a comb

on his desk like some secret hall pass.
And someone would say, *that's no comb, it's a knife*—
And it was. Like that the kid was gone. This past

haunts me now. I wonder, was it another life?
Was I another teacher then? Not true
every seven years all the old cells die.

Yes, some do, are born again and made new.
But others go on living to the end
just the same as they were. *Yes, in me, too,*

I think, fifteen years down the road. It bends
and I'm walking with the kids, memory
playing tricks; I sing with them those words again:

O land of the free by the Carib sea...
No tyrants here linger; despots must flee...

KNUCKLEHEAD LEARNS A NEW WORD

I'm sorry it wasn't till the end of the year
that I asked you to write about yourselves.

You filled pages in May and June, my arm
and wrist were sore from writing
wow and *oh my goodness* in the margins

as you shared stories from your lives,
about the times you fell in love
or lost somebody or learned to ride a bike.

And so many of you wrote about your mothers
as so many of the boys and girls I've taught since
have written about their mothers.

To my mother, for my mother. I've read these words
over and over for fifteen years and still
they move me. And that year, my first

time craning my neck to read them, I didn't
understand how holy it was, what I was doing,
holier than the masses I attended

at the mission, than the confessions I made or the readings
I assigned you: Dante and the Bible and *Huckleberry Finn.*
I wasted so many words and days, bleeding

the clock down, forcing your silence. When you broke it,
Ay Maestro! You would say. *Tell us something new.*
Now I can't remember anything I said. I remember

it felt strange not to know what word would come
next. I remember thinking I did not like
letting go control.

And on the radios blasting as I walked home I heard
Pasame la botella and you singing along

Voy a beber en nombre de ella
and whizzing by me too on the bikes

you'd long since learned to ride.
Ay Maestro! Ay Dante! you'd call out,

A smile and a laugh at my nickname
but yes, even the snicker's a grace, I realize now.

I don't have the yearbook anymore from '05-'06
but I bet some of you do, some of you

were on student council, right?
Put us back in touch.

I want more than regret
for my first seven months as your teacher,

want more than the cliché—*you gave me
more than I gave you*—that's not enough

though it's certainly true. There's another,
maybe better: *Words can travel a thousand miles.*

And what I'm thinking about now
is the 5 or 10 or 20

your mothers traveled for our first
parent teacher conferences. How nervous

I was, and did not know yet
how much you loved them.

For the Spanish speaking I knew enough
to say *es un privilegio a enseñar*

a su hijo. It is a privilege
to teach your son.

Even then, slow as I was to see
how holy it all was,

I saw that. *Privilegio.* I say it still
in Spanish that hasn't got much better,

to parents of boys and girls
who speak that tongue. *Es un privilegio.*

Privilegio. PRIV – IL – LAY – HEE – OH,
the word lighter in Spanish than English,

floating through tongue and teeth.
I learned it, among many other things,

my first year, with you.

LISTENING TO RICHARD ROHR IN THE
HOSPITAL DURING QUARANTINE

He says, *fall through your life situation*
into your life. I don't know what that means.
In a hospital bed, a tube drains pus and blood

from my infected elbow. In my other arm
an IV pumps a drug meant to clean
me out. This, I guess, is my life situation,

this failing body needing surgery
for the swelling, oxycodone for the pain,
Father Richard talking while the tube drains pus and blood

into the 'Wound Drainage Collector'—
all that badness in a bucket, what does it mean?
Will we fall together through this life situation,

my infection and me? And rediscover
life as if awakening from a dream?
Father Richard says, *look at that pus and blood,*

it's not just your sins pooling, it's everybody's,
not just you *needing oxycodone to sleep*
but everybody. Everybody falling through their life situations
into their lives, their pain, their pus and blood.

SOUTH MINNIE IS THE WORLD

Somebody wrote *PEOPLE LIVE HERE*
on the wood boarding up the windows.
They wrote *PLEASE DON'T BURN* and *GEORGE FLOYD*
    and I see fear
in those words. I see hope, too. I see light and shadow.

On the wood boarding up the windows
somebody else wrote *I CAN'T BREATHE* and *SAY HIS
    NAME.*
In those words I see hope, too. I see light and shadow.
On the street he was murdered I walk free. I feel shame.

Somebody else wrote *I CAN'T BREATHE* and *SAY HIS
    NAME.*
They shared those words so the world can see.
On the street he was murdered I walk free. I feel shame
I can't package into a post for friends to see.

They shared these words so the world can see
they understand *BLACK LIVES MATTER.*
I can't package into a post for my friends to see
Bodies break Flesh bleeds Bones shatter.

They understand *BLACK LIVES MATTER,*
write it on the wood boarding up the windows.
Bodies break. Flesh bleeds. Bones shatter.
In those words I see hope, too. I see light and shadow.

PUBLIC WORKS

We said "Streets" and they knew
what we meant, patching the cracks in the road,
pouring down fresh new tar, paving over
till the ground beneath us was smooth.

It is a public work—
what is more public than an avenue,
a street, a boulevard? But I always said
"Streets." And I hated the work.

One summer was enough,
taking the shit of a Lifer who felt
it was his mission to grind down college
boys who came, hands open—

"How can I help?" a go-to—
and when the Lifer explained, I would say
"okay," and try…and do it wrong, the truck
too far to the right or

The left, crack not blown
out enough, too much or too little spray.
And he'd explain again, I'd say "okay"
and "Good to know" and then

Do it wrong again. And
again. The Lifer grew upset with me,
would alternate between silent treatment
and straight-up yelling. I

Took it. I took it. I
wanted to quit so many times. But no
I wouldn't let him win.

Summer: hell together,
the Lifer and me, patching roads up and
down the city, his shitty classic rock
blaring, him jerking thumb

This way and that way, him
losing patience with me, me learning how
to say fuck you without saying the words:
I stand by the truck, I

Watch him work. I don't make
a move to help. I am eighteen years old.
I know nothing of the world except the
inside of the Public

Works truck. Summer pays for
college. Summer gives meaning to shovel,
to pour, to blow, to patch. I don't listen
though, to Lifer. I don't

See where he fits. Cosmic
faith requires his presence to have meaning;
I write these poems where he keeps showing up.
I can still see his eyes

Narrow in my rear view,
his hands raised in exasperation. He had
to survive me that summer, too, I know,
sheltered kid driving truck

For the first time, patching,
blowing, shoveling, letting the long hour
go without doing a damn thing, public
work or non-work while cars

Drove by and the world went
on. I never got used to working with
the Lifer and he never got used to
me, my last day a joy

For both of us. Lifer,
this poem is yours, a public work. I hope
it lasts longer than the streets we worked on,
my anger like a crack,

Blown out by the force of
time, twenty years of life telling me it
was meant to be, that summer you yelled and
yelled, and I took it; sealed.

Over, this poem, sprayed,
beyond revision. I don't want to open
afresh though I know streets, words, grow old and
I will see you again.

III

I watch, and am as a sparrow upon the housetop.

— Psalm 102:7

THE DAY NORMA STANISHA TOOK PITY ON ME

A day like any other in my
eighth grade life. Standing at my locker
alone in the morning. It was spring, I think,
this year of school almost over, this year
with its grey slacks and blue dress shirts, this year
with the countries and capitals of South
America I was memorizing and
the algebra I feared so much but then
came to understand, and the basketball games
I played, those brief blips when my body
knew what it was doing. How to turn and shoot
the baby hook. How to grab the rebound
and fire an outlet pass to Darius
on the wing. How to race down the court
after, to follow, chest burning, joyful.
All of that over now. Now in the hallway
of the ancient school, alone as usual
and Norma Stanisha approaching.

Probably it was a Friday and she'd planned
all her lessons. For once could look up from those
glasses that were always slipping down her
nose, could peer out into the hallway,
the wilderness of teenagers she had lived among
for so long…
   She liked my voice. When we read
stories in class, she would always pick me to
read them aloud, inviting me to the front
to sit near her desk and turn the pages
of a dog-eared Collected Works of Poe
or Washington Irving, or a poem by Frost.

I was her little favorite and didn't like it.
I didn't like it. And now here she was
in the hallway for maybe the first time all year
noticing me alone, realizing me alone.
I hated her more in that moment than
any other all year, hated her
approach, the clanking of her earrings,
the soft look of her eyes, hated the question
she asked. *Have you made many friends?*
I hated how her eyes got softer with my silence,
hated *there's more to school than studying,*
hated her reclusive heart climbing out of its cave.
                       But it is Friday now
twenty five years later, and she is gone,
and I have papers to grade like she did,
and my hair has gone gray like hers was,
and my students will laugh at me as hers did,
and very soon I know it will be my turn
to wait in the wings of the hallway,
to get ready to say the wrongest things,
the wrongest things there are to say.

BREAKING THE POCKET

We used to play our games
at Midway Stadium,
where the semi-pro baseball
team played, and scrambling, breaking
the pocket, I heard the *scritch
scratch* of sand beneath my cleats.
Downfield, no one was open,
or no one I could see,
so I was running, the blood
rushing through my body
so fast, and I was a boy
and there were men chasing me.

I never liked to slide
the way they taught me to
in practice, not because
I was brave or courageous
but because it didn't seem
fair. My running back, he took
the hits. Why shouldn't I?
And so I did, hit after
hit, the crunch of my body
into their bodies, the sand
of the infield scraping
my naked arms and elbows.

Back on the sidelines Coach would yell:
for not being patient,
for not sliding, or in other
moments, for throwing and hoping,
not knowing where the ball was going.

It's more than twenty years
ago but I can still see
him, the little froths of spit
at the corners of his mouth,
the way his whole body
shook with rage. If he could,
he said, *he* would go out there
and read the defense, make
the play. I wonder sometimes
if he thought because I wore
a helmet and shoulder pads
the anger pouring out
of him became a purer
drink somehow? as if football
distilled his frustration—
the stomping of his feet,
the throwing of his clipboard,
his head leaning far too close
to mine—like charcoal filtered,
like grapes crushed in a vineyard,
like this would be whiskey
or wine we'd all enjoy some day?
As if some day simply
watching a boy throw a football
to another, I could enjoy it
as simply as I could
the taste of a velvety
red or a smoky glass
of Knob Creek.

And where Midway Stadium
once stood is now an office
complex, row on row of them—
Energy Park Drive,

where once our old bus creaked
up to the stadium gates,
and we, silent in our pads
and helmets as if ready
for war, walking past our
classmates with their popcorn
and facepaint, knowing we
had found the real today.

What was Coach but general
and we but soldiers today?
And why would I think I
was any different, who
held the ball, who handed off
the ball, who threw it arcing
in a spiral down the field?
The blood pounded in my head
the same as in my teammates'.
We all heard Billy Joel
sing *You might be right. I*
might be crazy as we stretched
our teenage bodies under
the lights…and I am Coach's
age now myself. I teach kids
the same age I was then.

But it just might be a
lunatic you're looking for
resounds from those days
to this one, and I say
"Yes, yes." I put my helmet
on. I get the play from Coach.
My students write their poems,
their stories, their essays.

I read them all. I try to
say the helpful thing. I nod
my head. "Yes, Coach," I say.
"I got it. I got it,"
and jog back on to the field.

LEFT TO LOVE

for david

at the end of a summer
at the beginning of a school year
in the middle of a pandemic
in the where-are-we of a fight
for racial justice

a young man, an old student of mine, dies
there is no sense to it—
eighteen years old
class of 2020
he was eighteen
eighteen years old

"since the beginning of the pandemic"
"in the middle of the pandemic"
i say these words as if as if
in the pandemic's mouth as it closes
over me even grief is made
a little darker

i've thought of you father
you jesus follower
you poet
you priest

into the waters of the word
you have dived so many times
and let your eyes adjust
to seeing underwater

like peter who dived into the sea
and came up for air to talk
with the risen one

you said
he handed me a meal
and told me to feed
them until
            there is nothing
left to love

mama's voice
from raisin
that time she caught her falling son
and loved him like the jesus follower
she was too
there is always something left to love
she said

father
there is nothing left
of my student
but stories now
memories

i play the audio
of his college essay
that i find in my email
i hear him talk about his dream
of playing soccer in the pros
of making his family proud

he goes on and on
well past the limit

of six hundred and fifty words
and i am grateful for his breaking
the rules now
now there is a little more
of him
left to love

After Joseph Brown, SJ

THE BOY AT THE BIG UNIVERSITY

Minneapolis, 2002

The boy at the big university,
alone with his conservative past
walking through ice and snow with Chesterton
in his head. *The way to love anything
is to realize it might be lost.*
And the boy sees his faith that way, holds
it for the first time, takes two buses
every weekday second semester
from Dinkytown to the Cathedral
and says the prayers from his childhood—
Lord, I am not worthy to receive you
and *Our Father, who art in Heaven*
and kneels at the times that everybody
kneels, and stands at the times everybody stands.
Takes the wafer in his hand. Puts the wafer
in his mouth. Holds it there for a minute
on his tongue like the nuns have taught him.
Jesus, he prays, *give me faith.* And who knows
how many times these same words and actions
are repeated? as the winter turns to spring
and the boy becomes religious but remains
a boy for all that.

THE FIRST SNOWFALL IN MINNEAPOLIS

October, 2020

Never mind the pandemic,
the people we don't get to see.

Never mind the white that coats
leaves that are still green.

Never mind that winter came
early, or that a fog has crept over

my thoughts. In a Minnesota prison
they are having a poetry reading,

and I have twenty kids
I get to write a letter of recommendation for.

The virus that waits for us while we sleep
is unprecedented, but so is the poetry reading,

so are those twenty kids, young people making their way.
Never mind the buses that don't run this year,

never mind they won't wait with red ears
and red runny noses. Never mind we will have

small christmas, small thanksgiving. One bird
is bird enough for me. But what about the tents

on 42nd street, at MLK Park, now dusted with frost?
Or at Powderhorn or by the ballfields

of Nokomis? When the snow fell this morning
I didn't remember the people in the tents,

though later I looked up a story on my phone and learned
there are tents at Minnehaha Falls, too and that

the same group that got people hotels to stay in
in the summer is helping people

find hotels now. *ZAKAH*. From the Muslim word
meaning the obligation to give 2.5 percent of your earnings

to charity. Never mind what you think of religion—
this one or any other—bless those people helping people

find a home. Bless them in the cold, when the snow is staying.
Bless them now in October with this dark blue bruise hanging
over us this morning.

Never mind that bruise now. When the sun comes up
in an hour or so, it will be light. We will find our human voices

again. We will approach one another once more. The masks we
wear
don't cover our eyes. Never mind them. Mind the eyes.

The masks we wear can't mute our words. We can
still say *Hello*. And *How are you*? And *What*

do you need?

TEACHER WAITS

Reads the poems, picks
one for the kids to read
and discuss, waits for class to begin
on the screen in front of him,
waits for their voices to come in

to his ears, and maybe, if he's lucky,
their eyes to be seen by his.
It is a strange time, February,
2021. This day leans on the next one
of the calendar, and that day on the day

after that, and on some day in the future
there will be a pile-up of days:
all those things we meant to say
to people we've not seen or heard from
in so long. For now, Teacher waits

for his students. He likes this poem—
it has an inner and an outer life—
it is a sonnet about a student
in a school. It takes time
to read and understand.

So many ways to read! he thinks
and remembers his first time,
in his mouth the sounds
of words—*at bat that
cat.* Such pleasure in seeing and saying,

hold old bold told—the sounds never
got old. The eyes hold. Eyes hold

and carry for mouth to tell. Tell words.
Words get told. Oh. How bold to
say a word out loud! That was school.

Teacher thinks about the things
he might have done, the paths he might
have tried instead. But he does not regret
Teaching. He waits for his students.
When he sees one on his screen

he says, *Hello.*

LOVING

Loving the stillness
of early morning,
he accepts the way
his body slows down
in the afternoon.

Loving the courage
of the woman
he married,
he loves the fire
that she can make.

In himself.
In herself.

Sometimes watching her
sleep, he sees her
as she was,
a child of five
or six, the little
nose with its precious
breath, the little
heart pumping blood
for tonight and
tomorrow.

Sometimes watching her
is the only medicine
for him and his upset
soul, the child in him
who wants to matter

just a little more,
who wakes in the night,
who wants to be held
but struggles
to ask.

NOTHING REMAINS AS IT IS
Spring, 2021

Nothing remains as it is.
A scar changes the landscape
of skin, a murder the landscape
of a city. A place holds
what has happened there. That's why
everybody's holding their breath.

A place holds what has happened,
the common human actions—
trades of food or hammers and nails
for dollar bills and coins, or trades
of the same for things that change
the landscape of the body, make it strange:

I mean, a couple of times a week in the year George
        Floyd
was murdered a car would pull up in front
of our condo, would idle
in the street. Then someone would come
to the window of the car or else
yell up to the neighbor's window.

No, I never saw the thing that changed
hands. But we clicked on Zillow
for the two millionth time yesterday
and found a new home. Everybody's holding on
to something. Me? Nine blocks from
38th and Chicago, I hold my breath.
Then I let it go.

PRAYER FOR WHEN THE CITY OPENS

When the city opens, is there something
this citizen will know now that he has
not known before? When the city opens, gone,
this man. Gone, that woman. And this child, too: gone. It's wrong
to wring your hands about a shop but not these lives. Deep
calls to deep, they say in the Book. Deep within,
they say, is God. Ok, Still Small Voice, talk to me,
tell me how to be now in the new broken city, and
tell me what to say now to my new broken self. It gets
harder every day to say what I mean. The
secret to living well is to be simple, you say. Better
a man tie a millstone round his neck than lead one of
these little ones astray, you say, in the Book. Tell me,
Teacher, how to be a little one when the city opens every
door again. Let me walk through the ones you want me to, on time.

A Golden Shovel of Romans 7:20.

WHO ARE WE

the house sits and waits
on a street we've walked before

in a neighborhood with lots
of trees, by a park that sits

on bluffs above the river. who
are we to buy property? who

are we to make offers, promises
to pay this or that? who to

cover the gap between what is
appraised and what is agreed to?

our parents had some money
and now we have some money

and now we sit, our hearts
set on this beautiful home built

in 1890 where we can walk
a block and see the river

and the city glittering at night.
who? who? who? i keep asking

the question, owl that i am
not able to believe the gift is real.

NOTE ON ACTS 5

Still the sweat from yesterday.
Still the cuts from folding boxes
and packing them, and taping them shut.
Still cuts on my knuckles and fingers.

Still an ache in the small
of my back. And in the Acts
of the Apostles one couple
holds back some money

from the land they sold.
They keep it for themselves.
Give some to Peter
but somehow he knows.

Ananias and
Sapphira. They die
on the spot. The lesson,
I guess, is all land

is God's, ours for only
a moment. Still, it seems
harsh. They gave *something*,
didn't they? But not all.

God knows I don't
give all. I hold back
all the time. And Peter?
Mr. We Have Given

Up Everything To Follow
You? Well, when the chips
were down, he ran and hid.
So…it doesn't seem

fair for poor Ananias
and Sapphira, tithing some
but not all, and dying.
Still, I get it.

I get it in my gut.
I get "don't hold back."
I get "give everything and follow."
I get "what's mine is yours."

Yes, I could be very good
in a cult. I have been
very good in a cult. I am
Catholic and have been all kinds:

I've prayed the beads.
I've walked the stations.
I've whispered words to
you, God, and not known

what they mean. I have
stuttered out of my child's
mouth "righteousness," "grace,"
"mortal sin." I have nodded

off at mass and let
the pew knock my knees
awake. Ananias did
his deed "with the full

knowledge of his wife."
Why both he and Sapphira
dropped dead before
Saint Peter. O God,

some preacher somewhere
is taking this text
to a crowd of people, is
wrapping arms

around it, cradling it
like I hold the last
bit of things from the fridge
after everything else is gone.

There are no more boxes
left to hold things so
I empty the bag with the
packing blankets and stuff

it full of bottles—
salad dressing, sauces and mayo.
I hold that lumpy thing
in my arms like a baby

and carry it to our car.
Exegesis, like moving,
is messy. Things break
in time, and translation.

NOTES

"Knucklehead's Regrets" is a *low-coup*, a form playing with the haiku and innovated by Amiri Baraka.

"left to love" is modeled after and in conversation with "The Shore: Peter Remembers" by Father Joseph Brown, SJ.

ACKNOWLEDGMENTS

These poems have been inspired and nourished by real people and real communities. I hope to name as many of those as I can and beg forgiveness for any I forget:

First, and most importantly, thank you, Cristina. Your daily embodying of beauty in word and deed, and your willingness to speak up for justice inspire me.

Thank you, Andrew, for life-long friendship and reading and engaging with this collection from its earliest days to its completion.

Thank you, Mom, Dad, and brothers Adam, Nathan, and Jared. Your witness to love in big and small ways inspires me, and without that love, I wouldn't have been able to write these poems.

Thank you, faculty and staff at Cristo Rey Jesuit High School-Twin Cities for regularly inspiring me with your kindness, love, and compassion as educators.

Thank you, students I've had the privilege to teach at Cristo Rey—your lives and your stories nourish me, give me hope on the daily.

Thank you especially student members of Cristo Rey's Poetry Club—some of the poems in this collection are in conversation with your own life-giving poems!

Thank you, first students I ever taught at Mt. Carmel High School in Benque, Belize. It's a cliché, but whatever: you taught me more than I taught you. And also, you taught me how to *be* a teacher.

Thank you, Mariam Pera, for friendship and championship of both poetry and community when I've needed both.

Thank you, Deborah Keenan, for mentoring me through doubts and my failing-to-say-what-I-want-to-say drafts. You've taught and continue to teach me how to be a poet.

Thank you, Father Brown, for mentorship as a teacher and poet, and collaborating in innovative and traditional ways with my students. Your presence in my (and my students' lives) is a godsend.

Thanks to the good people of Rutgers Institute for Racial Justice, especially workshop leaders, Gregory Pardlo and Airea Dee Matthews. Your leadership on the 2021 Anti-Racist Writing Retreat helped clarify key sections of this manuscript.

Thanks to all the poets and writers who were generous enough to humor my pandemic-induced #poetrylockdown webseries (2020-2021) and / or commune with students in big and small ways. Your witness on and off the page inspire me, and without you, this book wouldn't exist. So, thank you, Ariane Sandford, Isha Camara, Spencer Reece, Kai Coggin, Katrina Vandenberg, Michael Kleber-Diggs, Teri Cross-Davis, Phillip Metres, Dana Gioia, Eric Gamalinda, Ladan Osman, Deborah Appleman, and Zeke Caligiuri.

Big thank you to the passionate Pauline scholarship and writing of Sarah Ruden, N.T. Wright, Fr. Richard Rohr, and Emmanuel Carrere. Your work and your studious imaginations have nourished and fired my own.

Thank you, Maceo Montoya, for a decade-plus of collaborations and conversations with the Cristo Rey community and for the beautiful and provocative cover art that converses with these poems.

Thank you, Norton Stillman, John Toren, and all the good people at Nodin Press, for your careful, thoughtful work in helping bring these poems into the world.

Finally, thank you, Reader, whoever you, wherever you are. Without you, this book doesn't happen.

Zach Czaia has worked as a teacher for fifteen years, and currently teaches English at Cristo Rey Jesuit High School in Minneapolis, MN. His first book, *Saint Paul Lives Here (In Minnesota)*, was published in 2015. To learn more about Zach and his thoughts and writings on poetry, faith, teaching, and all things knucklehead, follow him on Twitter @ czaiazach.

Made in the USA
Lexington, KY
07 February 2017